Amazing Bikes

WRITTEN BY
TREVOR LORD

PHOTOGRAPHED BY
PETER DOWNS

[DK]

DORLING KINDERSLEY
London · New York · Stuttgart

A Dorling Kindersley Book

Project editor Louise Pritchard
Art editor Mark Regardsoe
Managing editor Sophie Mitchell
Managing art editor Miranda Kennedy
Production Shelagh Gibson

Illustrations by Bruce Hogarth and Julie Anderson
Bikes supplied by Bike UK (pp 26/27); Peter Burls (pp 20/21); Mike Burrows (pp 12/13);
Barry Eastman (pp 14/15); Mark Hall Cycle Museum, Harlow Council (pp 8/9, 18/19);
Museum of Mankind (pp 22/23); Les Nash (pp 24/25); Oddball Juggling Company (pp 28/29);
Science Museum (pp 10/11); Swallow Cycles, Essex (pp 16/17)
Special thanks to Streetbike Drag Club; Dudley Hubbard for photography pp 22/23;
Adrian Whicher for photography pp 10/11; Phil Gatwood for photography pp 12/13;
David Fung and James Pickford for research

First published in Great Britain in 1992 by
Dorling Kindersley Limited
9 Henrietta Street, London WC2E 8PS

A CIP catalogue record for this book
is available from the British Library

ISBN 0-86318-892-3

The author would like to dedicate this book to Louise

Colour reproduction by Colourscan, Singapore
Printed in Italy by A. Mondadori Editore, Verona

Contents

These children are about 1.2 m tall. They will show you the size of the bikes in the main pictures.

First bicycles

The first bicycles came in all shapes and sizes. Some of the early ideas are still used today, but many, not surprisingly, were used only once.

Cross-section of Dunlop's tyre

Strips of sailcloth

Rubber coating

Air-filled inner tube

Riding on air
In 1888 John Dunlop was the first person to fit an air-filled tyre to a bicycle. His idea changed the whole look of bicycles – not to mention their comfort and speed.

Cord attached to the brake. The brake was worked by winding this cord around the handlebars

Swinging along
A swing bicycle was made in 1887. To make it go forwards, the two riders pulled down on levers to swing the basket. This made the bicycle roll along.

Up and over
Mounting a penny-farthing takes practice. The rider puts one foot on the step, uses the other foot to scoot the bike forwards, then stands up on the step and vaults into the saddle. Easy!

Tyres made of solid rubber

No knees
In the 1890s most men wore jackets and knee-length trousers for cycling. Women wore rationals, which were trousers carefully designed so as not to show the knees.

Coining a name

This bicycle was nicknamed the penny-farthing because its big and little wheels reminded people of two British coins of the day – the penny and the farthing. Its proper name is an ordinary. There were many different kinds of ordinaries. This one was made in 1871.

Footrest for use when speeding downhill

A long walk

Hobby-horses were used in the early 1800s. They did not have pedals. The rider sat on the saddle and moved the bike by running along.

Boneshakers

The boneshaker of the late 1860s was an early bicycle with pedals. It had a metal frame and metal tyres on wooden wheels. It was uncomfortable to ride – which is how it got its name.

First motorbikes

It is often forgotten that motorbikes have existed for as long as cars – over 100 years. They have improved since the early days!

Slipping and sliding

The early motorbikes had poor tyres and a heavy engine fixed high up on the frame. This made them liable to slide sideways on the bad roads.

Lazy cyclist

One man could not find a small enough engine to fit on his bicycle. So he fixed an engine on a trailer behind his bike, which pushed him along.

Mudguard holds over 22 litres of water

Container for coke

Firebox and boiler

Instant power

In the early 1900s it was very easy to turn a bicycle into a motorcycle. A wheel, with an engine to drive it, was simply bolted on to the side of the bicycle.

Hot seat

Gottlieb Daimler, one of the inventors of the car, made the first true motorcycle in 1885 before he made a car. His son rode for 8 miles (13 km) on it – in spite of the saddle catching fire!

Box for carrying equipment

Room for two

Single-seater motorcycles were made more sociable with the addition of a sidecar. The first sidecars were made of wickerwork and gave little protection to the passengers.

Front brake works directly on the tyre

Bone burner

In 1869 Sylvester Roper put a steam engine on to a boneshaker bicycle. The saddle was close to the hot engine, so riding the bike must have been even more uncomfortable than riding an ordinary boneshaker.

Steamed up

This steam-powered motorcycle was made in 1889. Small pieces of coke were burnt to heat water to make the steam. The coke and water were kept in special containers within the cycle frame.

Bicycle sport

The first known bicycle race took place in 1868. Today there are many kinds of bicycle races, and some unusual bicycle sports too.

Race for gold
First run in 1903, the Tour de France race covers 2,500 miles (4,020 km) and lasts three weeks. At the start of each stage the overall leader is given a yellow jersey to wear.

Brakes are operated by turning the right handlebar

Pedalled ponies
Bicycles make good substitutes for ponies in a game of polo. Bicycles are cheaper and the riders do not have so far to fall!

Wheel fork has a blade on only one side of the wheel

Fast swordsmen
Cycling and fencing skills were needed in ring-taking races which took place in Germany about 90 years ago. The cyclists raced around a track collecting rings on a sword.

Cross riders
Mud, streams, grass, and ditches are all tackled by cyclo-cross competitors. Sometimes the muddy hills are so steep that the riders have to dismount and carry their bikes up.

Tough sport

A triathlon is a cycle race with a difference. The competitors swim, then cycle, and then run – without a break. Some races take over eight hours.

Built for speed

This modern racing bike was designed by its rider for speed. It is the only one of its kind. It has no steel tubing, as ordinary bikes have, but a one-piece frame made of carbon fibre and filled with foam.

Help from the bank

Track racing takes place on oval tracks with steep sides which the cyclists can use to help them go faster. The bikes have one gear and no brakes. The riders slow down or stop by pedalling slower.

Solid wheel cuts through the air better than a spoked wheel

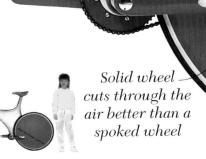

Motorbike sport

Some motorbike sports are fast, others are slow. Some take place in a stadium, others in the middle of a desert. All of them require skill and courage.

Keep it steady

Drag bikes race in twos on a track only ¼ mile (400 m) long. The riders lean forwards on their bikes to keep the front wheel down. "Wheelie bars" are fixed on the back to stop the bike spinning over backwards.

Fun in the sand

One of the hardest races is the Paris (France)-Cape Town (South Africa) rally. The three-week race goes through the Sahara desert. In spite of the sand and the heat, riders reach speeds of over 100 mph (160 km/h).

Short burst

A drag bike starts and accelerates very quickly, reaching a speed of 200 mph (320 km/h) in seven seconds. At the end of a race the rider takes ½ mile (800 m) to slow down and stop!

BARRY EASTMA

1320   CBX

1,320-cc engine

7.5-cm-wide front tyre

Left only

Speedway riders race around a track. They always race anti-clockwise, so the bikes only turn left. Just as well – they cannot go right as the footrest would hit the ground!

Cool customers

In some countries a popular motorbike sport is ice racing. Long spikes are screwed into the tyres of the bikes so that they can grip the slippery ice.

Scraped knees

Motorbike racers lean over so far on the corners that their knees touch the ground. They wear "knee sliders" for protection.

On the rocks

The sport called "trials" tests the skills of balancing and handling a bike. Among other things, riders have to drive over rocks and tree trunks – and they are not allowed to put their feet down.

Rider has no seat

Tokyo Express

CB37 Racing

33-cm-wide back tyre

Out of the ordinary

You will not see these machines on every street corner. They are specially built to be different. Some are so different they are the only one of their kind.

Solar energy
People who get tired easily may like a bicycle like this. *Sunpower* has a solar-powered electric motor which can be turned on for extra power – especially useful when pedalling uphill!

Tyre change
This bike can be pedalled on land and water. It floats on water with its wide tyres, and for travelling on land it has tyres with ordinary bike tyres attached round them.

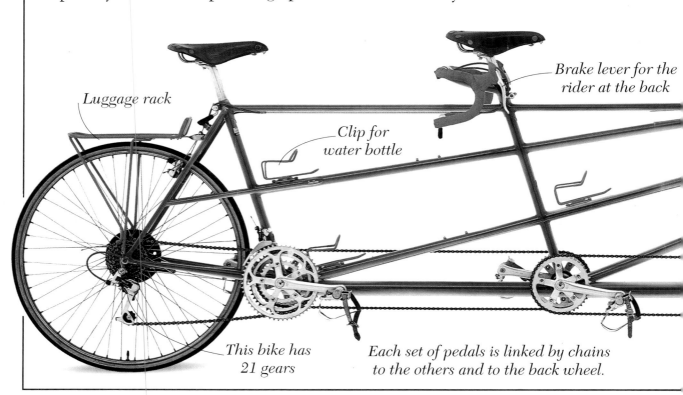

Luggage rack

Clip for water bottle

Brake lever for the rider at the back

This bike has 21 gears

Each set of pedals is linked by chains to the others and to the back wheel.

Made to measure

In the 50s and 60s people in the USA "chopped up" their bikes and added new bits to make "choppers". Choppers have long front forks and high handlebars.

Green bike

The Ecomobile has only two wheels but is enclosed in a body like a car. It can go at over 160 mph (250 km/h) but it uses less petrol than a car and takes up less room on the road too!

Balancing act

This "bike" was made in the early 1900s. It had a huge spinning wheel called a gyroscope (*jie-roe-scope*) between the two passenger compartments. This worked like a spinning top to stop the vehicle from falling over when it was standing still.

Sharp corners

Bicycle wheels are always round, right? Wrong! Circus performers sometimes ride bikes with square wheels!

Luggage holder

Bicycle built for three

In 1989 three British army members rode this triple-tandem bike 5,000 miles (8,046 km) across the USA from New York to Cupertino in California. Their eventful trip took 11 weeks.

Three-wheelers

Bikes that have three wheels are called tricycles. They are not made only for young children to ride – tricycles have many different uses.

Terrific trike
In 1896 a giant tricycle was made in the USA. The two back wheels had a diameter of 3.5 m and it took eight people to pedal the machine.

Sociable outing
Two people sitting side by side is a sociable, or friendly, way to travel, and this kind of tricycle is known as a sociable. The different-sized wheels on this 1880s model are like those of the penny-farthing so perhaps it should have been called a two-penny farthing!

Back wheels tilted towards each other

Handlebars

Rider lay back in the seat

Wheel chair

Tricycles help people with disabilities to get about. Some models are made to be "pedalled" by hand instead of by foot.

Car or bike?

With a chain, and the engine and back wheel of a motorbike, this Morgan three-wheeler is as much a motorcycle as it is a car. Said to have the speed of a motorcycle and the comfort of a car, it is known as a cyclecar.

Three-seater

A tricycle is useful for shopping trips. This one has two seats for children and space underneath for the shopping. And with three wheels to balance on, no-one has to step off at red traffic lights!

Cyclops

Restricted view

Cyclops was built in 1986 to be the fastest human-powered vehicle, but it failed. It – and its rider – were enclosed in a fibreglass body. The rider used an eye-doctor's instrument to see out – through a tiny hole in the front of the body.

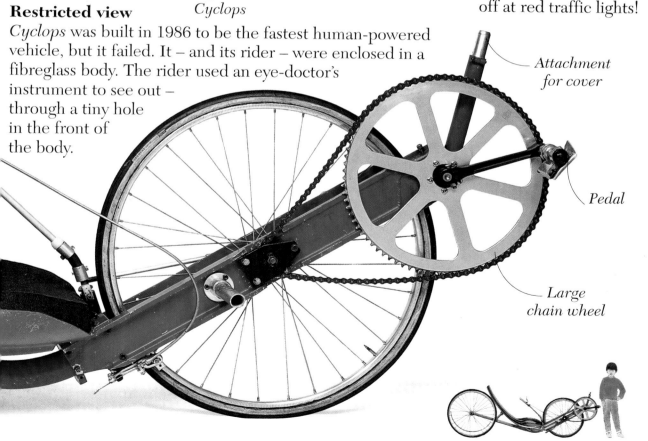

Attachment for cover

Pedal

Large chain wheel

Scooters

Scooters and mopeds are small, light, and cheap to run. Most of them cannot go as fast as motorbikes, but they are still great fun to ride.

Mass production
This extra-large Vespa scooter was made for publicity at a bike show. Proper Vespas were first made in 1947 and are now the third most-produced motor vehicles ever.

From water to land

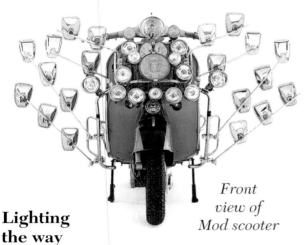

In 1952 Georges Monneret crossed the English Channel from Calais to Dover on a scooter. The scooter was mounted on floats and had a propeller driven by the back wheel. When Monneret landed at Dover, he took off the floats and rode the scooter to London.

Brake pedal

223·ARK

Front view of Mod scooter

Lighting the way

If you were a "Mod" in Britain during the 1960s, you had to have a scooter. And the more lights and mirrors it had, the more fashionable it was. There are many fans of Mod scooters today. This Mod scooter has 17 lights and 20 mirrors!

Dropped from the sky
In the Second World War small scooters were dropped by parachute for some of the soldiers. They were dropped folded up inside containers.

Standing room only
Some of the first scooters, like this autoped of 1916, were just copies of a child's scooter with an engine attached. Like the children's version, they were ridden standing up.

Pedal power
In some countries you have to wear a helmet on a motorbike but not on a moped. In Florida, USA, the rider of an old, but powerful, Harley-Davidson motorbike persuaded a police officer that he didn't have to wear a helmet – his bike had pedals, so it was really a moped!

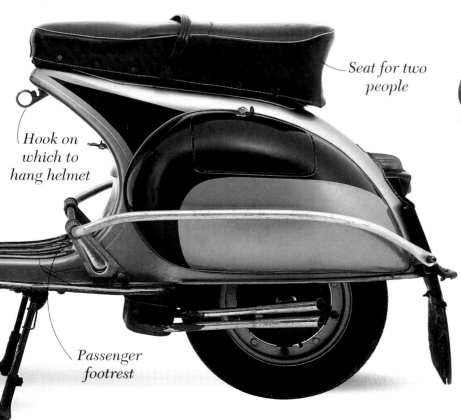

Seat for two people

Hook on which to hang helmet

Passenger footrest

On and off
A moped is like a bicycle with an engine. On this French moped the engine turns a roller which is touching the front wheel. When the moped is standing still, the engine is lifted off the wheel.

Bikes at work

Bicycles and motorbikes are not ridden just for fun. Many have a tough working life.

Emergency!
In some cities ambulance staff use motorbikes. The bikes carry the same equipment as ambulances do but can get to the scene of an accident sooner.

Message on a bike
As long ago as 1911, the British Post Office used motorbikes for delivering mail. This one is a Rover – a manufacturer which later became famous for its cars.

Sight for sore eyes
Some onion sellers in France cycle around with strings of onions on their handlebars. And to please tourists they often dress in traditional French costume.

Ice bike
Since 1922, tricycles have been used to sell ice-cream. Some can still be seen on hot days with their "cool box" on the front.

Street cleaner
This unusual bike is used in some cities to keep the streets clean. If a dog makes a mess, the "pooper scooter" comes and clears the mess away.

No problem
In some countries, people use bicycles far more than cars. They are able to carry all sorts of things in the basket without overbalancing.

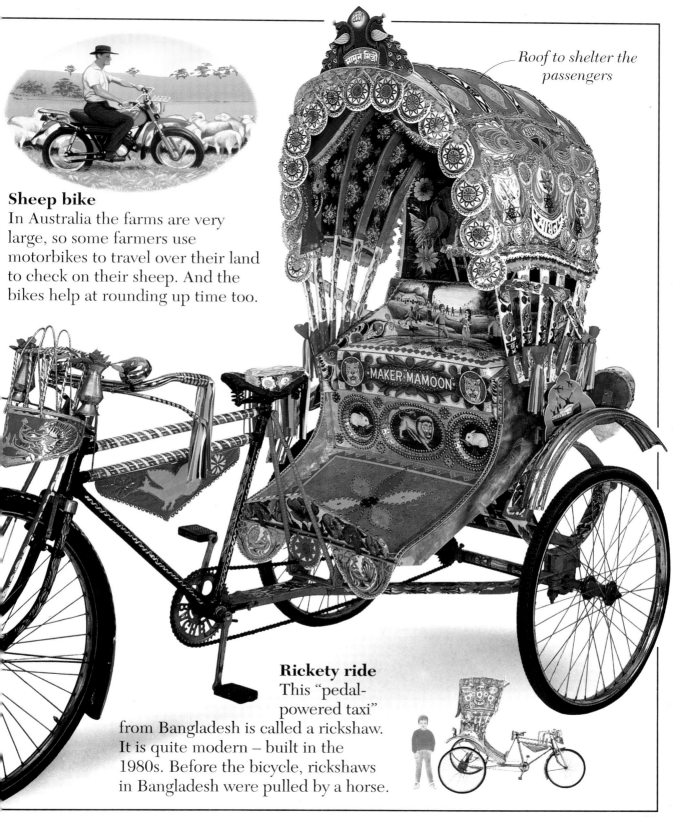

Sheep bike

In Australia the farms are very large, so some farmers use motorbikes to travel over their land to check on their sheep. And the bikes help at rounding up time too.

Roof to shelter the passengers

MAKER MAMOON

Rickety ride

This "pedal-powered taxi" from Bangladesh is called a rickshaw. It is quite modern – built in the 1980s. Before the bicycle, rickshaws in Bangladesh were pulled by a horse.

For the record

The excitement of being the fastest or the longest, the slowest or the biggest, leads people to do some extraordinary things.

Flashed past
The American Donald Vesco set the motorcycle world speed record in 1978. His bike *Lightning Bolt* had two engines and reached a speed of over 318 mph (512 km/h).

Bicycle made for 35
The bicycle with the most seats was made in Belgium. It is 20.4 m long and carries 35 riders. The bike weighs more than 1 tonne – over 60 times the weight of a normal bike.

Made it!
This is the longest motorbike in the world. It is 3.8 m long from the front tyre to the end of the frame at the back (not including the towing hook). The bike was handmade in six weeks – for a bet!

Back wheel from a Jaguar car

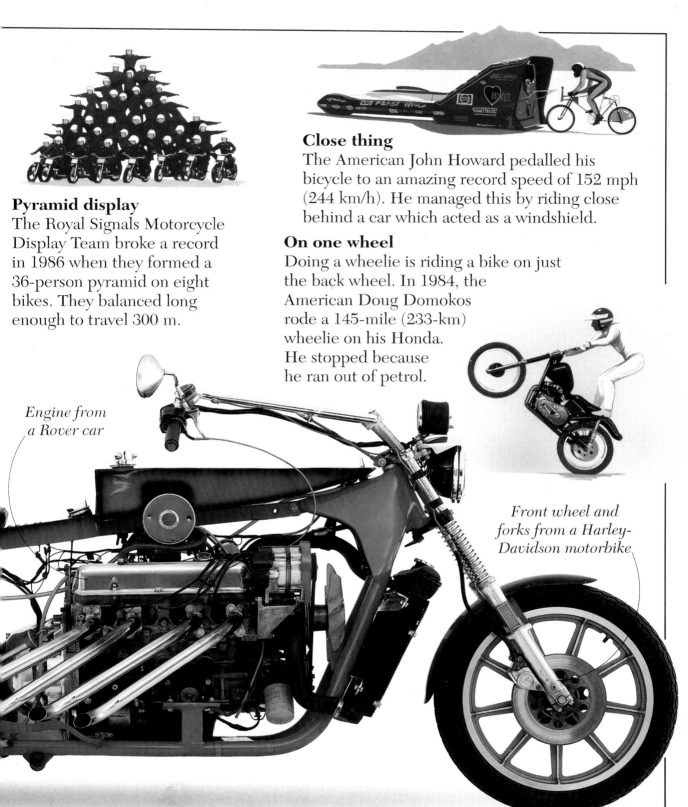

Pyramid display

The Royal Signals Motorcycle Display Team broke a record in 1986 when they formed a 36-person pyramid on eight bikes. They balanced long enough to travel 300 m.

Close thing

The American John Howard pedalled his bicycle to an amazing record speed of 152 mph (244 km/h). He managed this by riding close behind a car which acted as a windshield.

On one wheel

Doing a wheelie is riding a bike on just the back wheel. In 1984, the American Doug Domokos rode a 145-mile (233-km) wheelie on his Honda. He stopped because he ran out of petrol.

Engine from a Rover car

Front wheel and forks from a Harley-Davidson motorbike

On your bike

We may have supersonic aircraft, high-speed trains, and fast, comfortable cars, but for some journeys, the best way to travel is still by bike.

Cycle for health

Many people use an exercise bicycle to get fit. It can be made hard or easy to pedal, and a meter shows how fast and how far you are pedalling – even though you stay in one spot.

Family fun

Bikes are made for people of all ages. Children's bikes and baby seats let whole families take to the road – sometimes all on the same bike.

Quick-release clamp for speedy adjustment of the height of the saddle

Modern design

Bicycle designs are always changing. New ideas to make bicycles go faster and be more comfortable to ride are being tried out all the time.

Out in the wilds

A mountain bike can be ridden on almost any kind of ground. This means the rider can explore off the roads, away from other people and traffic.

21 gears

Off to work

Many people bicycle to work, as it is cheaper than going by bus or train. And on today's busy roads bicycling is often quicker than taking the car. Some towns and cities have special lanes for bicycles so that cyclists have an easier and safer journey. For safety it is best to always wear a helmet.

Safe not sorry

Cycle training teaches young cyclists how to ride safely. There is a lot to learn, from bicycle control and repair to road signs and traffic laws.

Gear lever on the handlebars within easy reach

Water bottle

ALUMINUM

TREK

Tyres with thick tread for travelling off-road

Watery grave

People in Amsterdam, Holland, dump their old bicycles in an unusual place – the canals. Two dredgers take 10,000 bicycles out of the canals every year. It takes them two years to clear all the canals, and then they have to start again!

Stunts and thrills

From circuses and showgrounds to specially filmed stunts, bikes of all types are used to create exciting spectacles. The riders have to be skilful – and brave.

Unicycle with two wheels

One or two wheels

A unicycle, a cycle with only one wheel and no handlebars, is very difficult to ride. Luckily, this one can be changed into a two-wheeler for the most difficult acts.

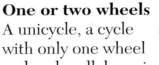

Circus trick

Some circus performers use unicyles. They juggle or catch and balance things on their head at the same time as controlling the bike – a trick best left to the experts.

Missed the bus

Eddie Kid was 16 when he jumped over 13 double-decker buses on his motorbike in 1976. At the time it was a world record.

An Evel job

Evel Knievel claims to have broken every bone in his body trying his famous motorcycle stunts. He once used a rocket-powered bike to try to leap 500 m across Snake River Canyon in the USA. His parachute opened too soon and Evel floated down into the canyon.

Step by step

Many crazy stunts have been done on a bicycle. One of the craziest was cycling down the steps of the Eiffel Tower in Paris, France – all 1,710 of them!

Team work

Motorcycle display teams perform exciting and often dangerous routines. They have many practice sessions together so that every member of the team does exactly the right thing at the right time.